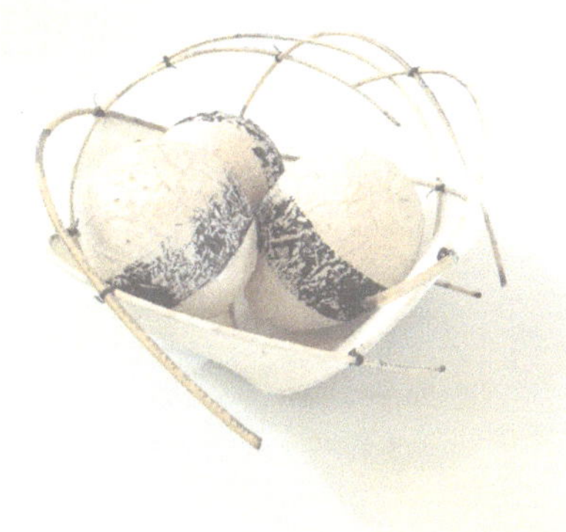

solitude

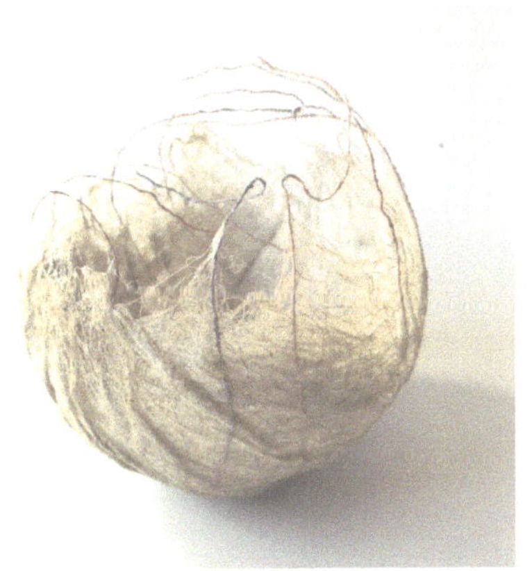

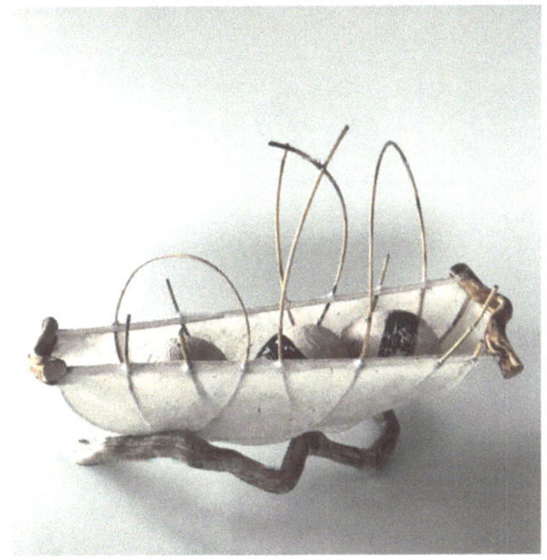

solitude

jacqueline mallegni

shanti arts publishing
brunswick, maine

solitude

published by shanti arts publishing

shanti arts llc
193 hillside road
brunswick, maine 04011
www.shantiarts.com

printed in the united states of america

cover: reflection • *ink wash on paper* • 2016

isbn: 978-1-947067-27-1

when there is nowhere
that you have determined
to call your own,
then no matter where you go
you are always home.

— muso soseki

2.22.15

the desert
a reprimanding mother
ecosystems
rock people’s sound
a breath

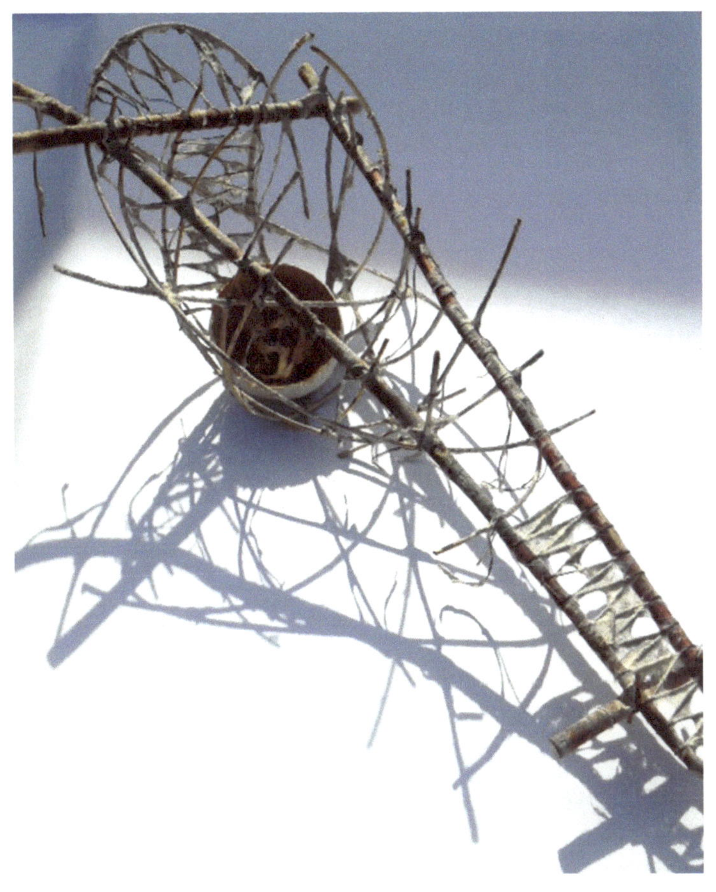

wind + thorns • *tamarisk, rattan, paper pulp, waxed linen* • 2015

3.20.15

grey sky pink dirt
yellow grass black rock
lichen
sip of chai birds fly

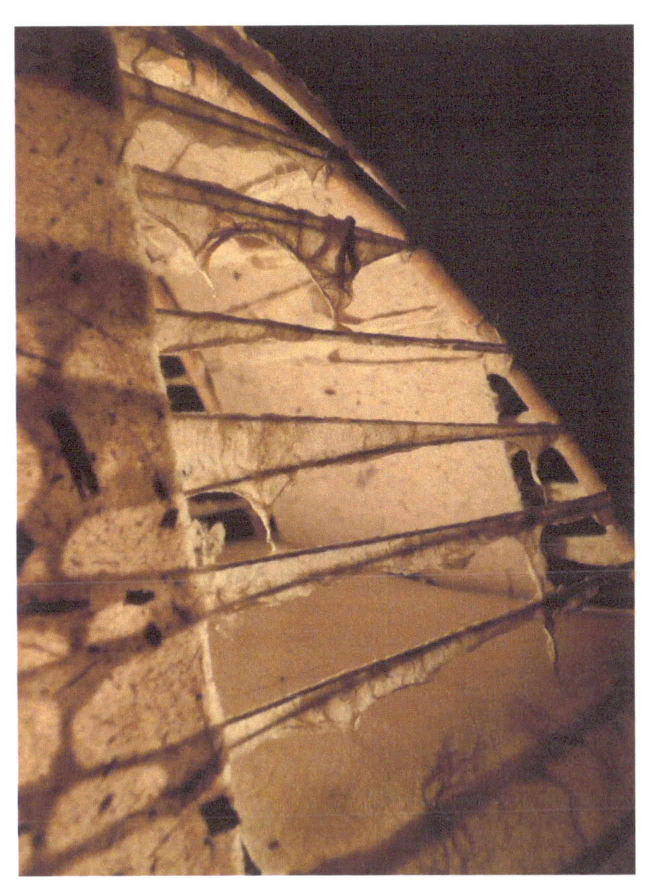

lantern detail • 2014

1.4.16

the words slip past my mind so quickly
warm winter sun
sit down for a moment
reflect on the beauty of things

orange slices dipped into warm chocolate
with butter
morgan's birthday cake makings
why isn't his wife making him a cake
why didn't she think of it

oh my
i get to be mom
how cool is that

do I want to

who is she now
without the skin and raven hair
that heart shaped ass

aches and pains in and out

like the word
poof gone

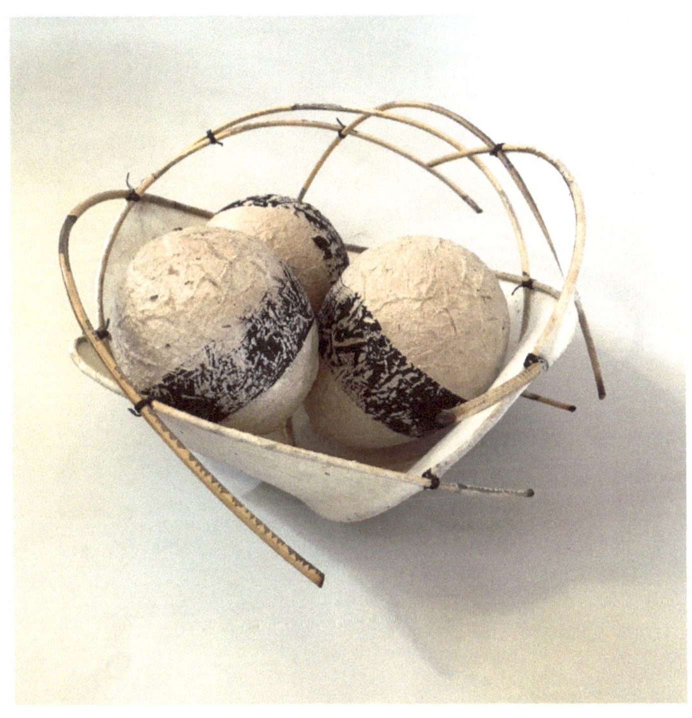

nest • *rattan, washi, waxed linen thread, cast paper, ink* • 2015

2.22.16

warm sun cottonwoods
a hint of green emerging
distant mountain snow

sandy desert floor
reviving sound of water
what a nice surprise

winter ice melting
snow melt along a creek bed
friends along the path

gurgling snow melt
remnants of winter linger
gathering birds sing

brilliant blue they wait

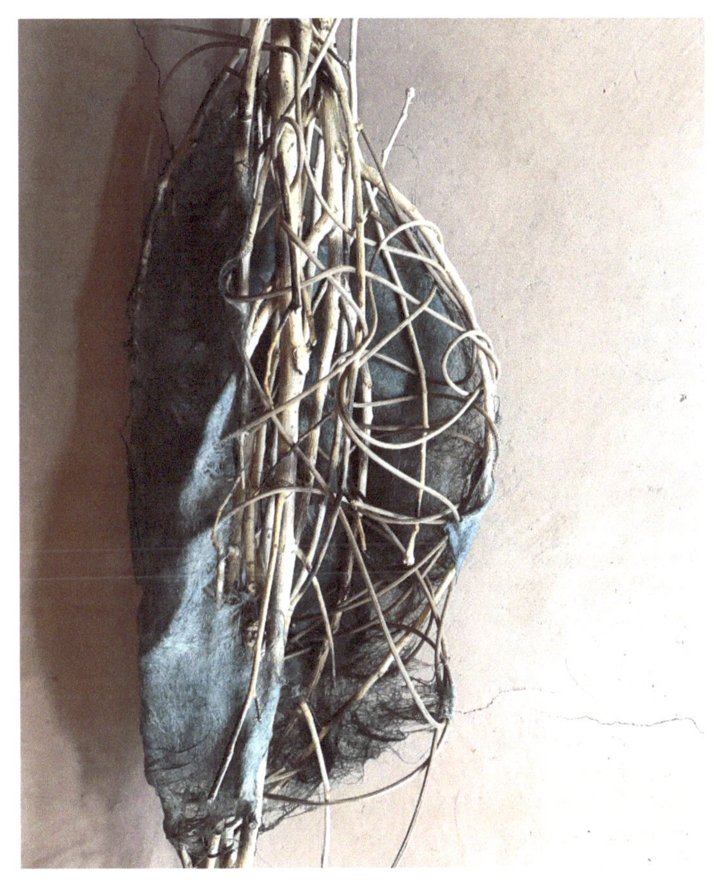

waterways • *cottonwood, flax, indigo* • 2017

3.16.16

sound of winter thaw
bubbles beneath thin ice
puppy feels freedom

journey • *rattan, willow, paper pulp, washi, waxed linen* • 2014

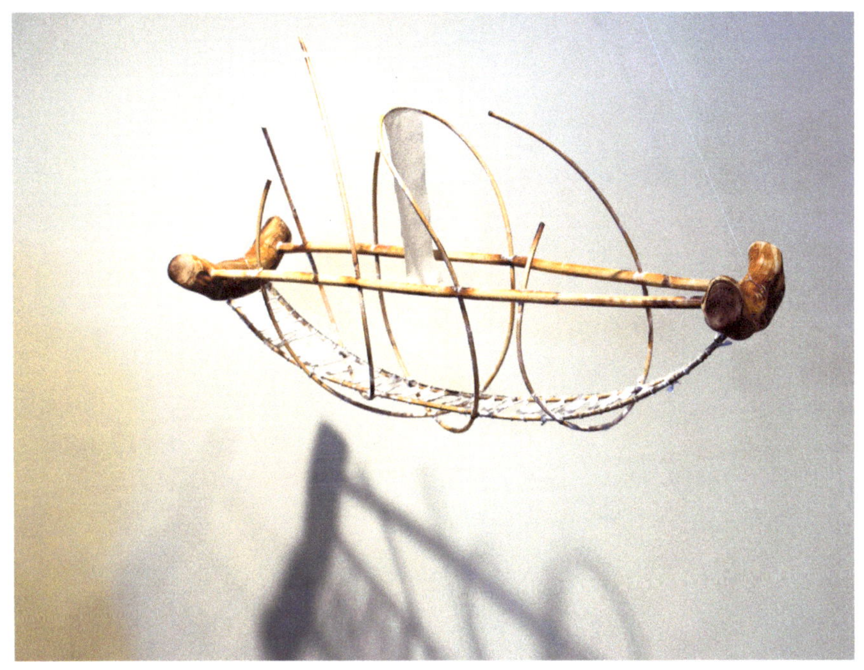

4.13.16

cumulus nimbus
water released in the sky
red earth shines in stone

tiny green circles
cottonwood leaves soon to burst
calm scent of red earth

words no words wanderer
spaces between no knowing
openness of mind

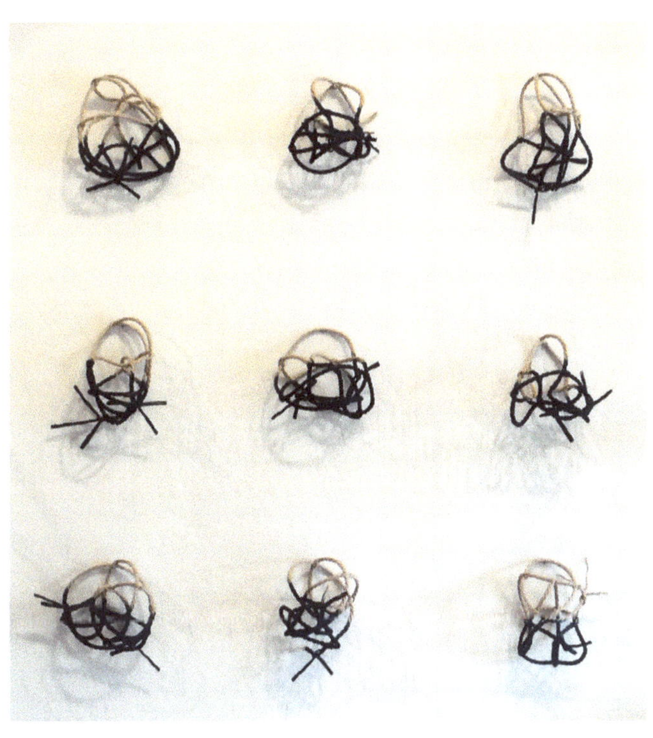

pattern language • *danish cord, indigo* • 2016

4.14.16 :: bloodlines

surreal is the landscape
dotted yellow and green
an occasional fuchsia
the road to santa fe is long
getting out
reflection
who is she really
sisters
who are they
what does that mean
sisters
family
their story lives in me
I don’t want it
just like I don’t want this drive through infertile
land
vega, a fertile valley
oh those Vega’s
mean and drunk
. . .

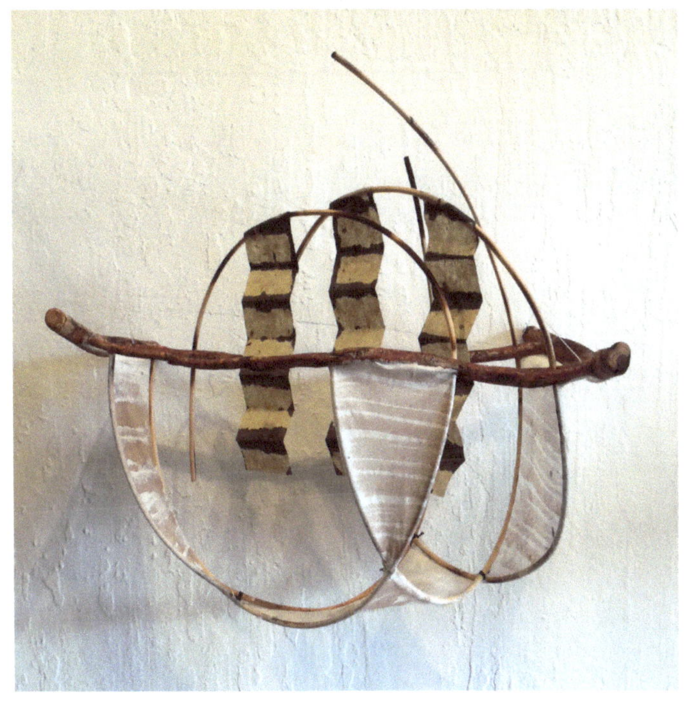

sisters' journey • *rattan, willow, ink, waxed linen thread* • 2016

. . .

abused daughters and grandmothers
no wonder she ran away
she didn't want to see their story in her

only her heart bleeds now
ovum spent on men that didn't care
like spikes
memories that sting
from that time where the reflection was too painful
it was not her story
now that's all she sees
what story does the son see
will he make up his own story
only to return to the one he ran away from

full circle
a new breath
a new miracle

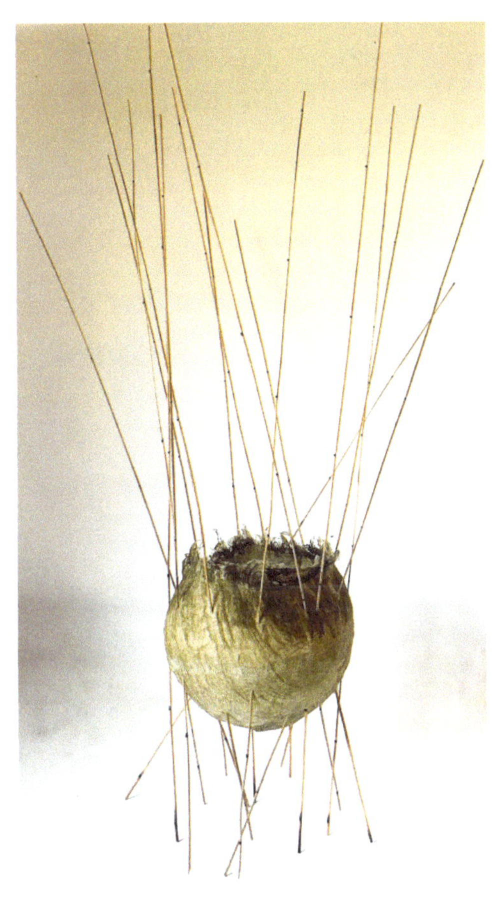

the meeting pool • *cast flax, encaustic medium, reed* • 2017

11.29.16

squeaky snow tracks shine
paw prints glide along the path
soul cleaning soft air

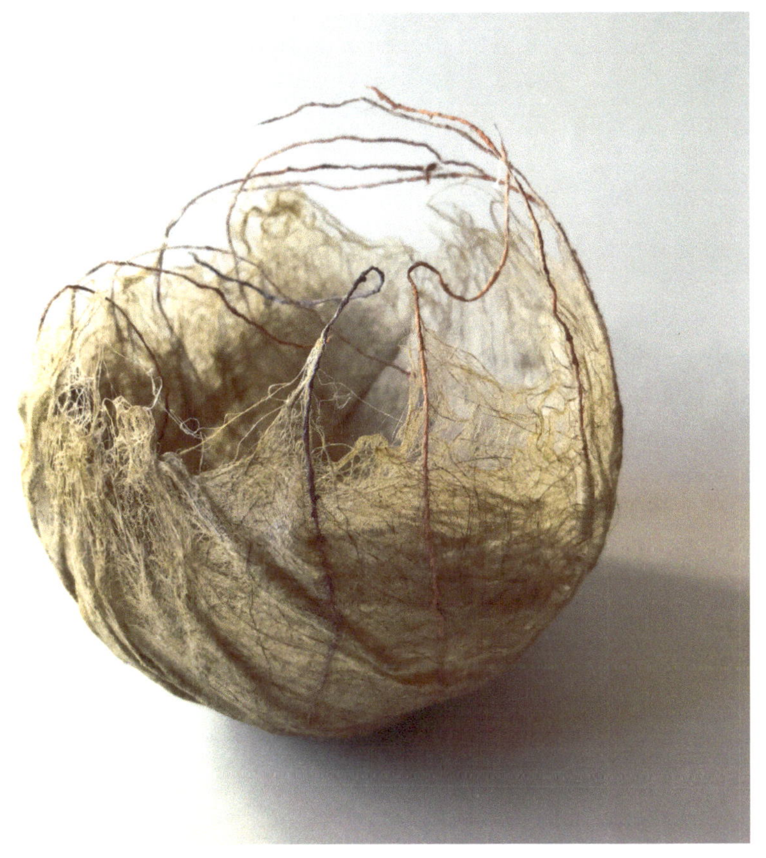

pod • *flax, silk* • 2017

12.11.16

a walk with aspens
water trees mountains and snow
eagle wings pass by

prayers for water/water to prayers

tamarisk, rattan, washi, monoprint • 2013-2016

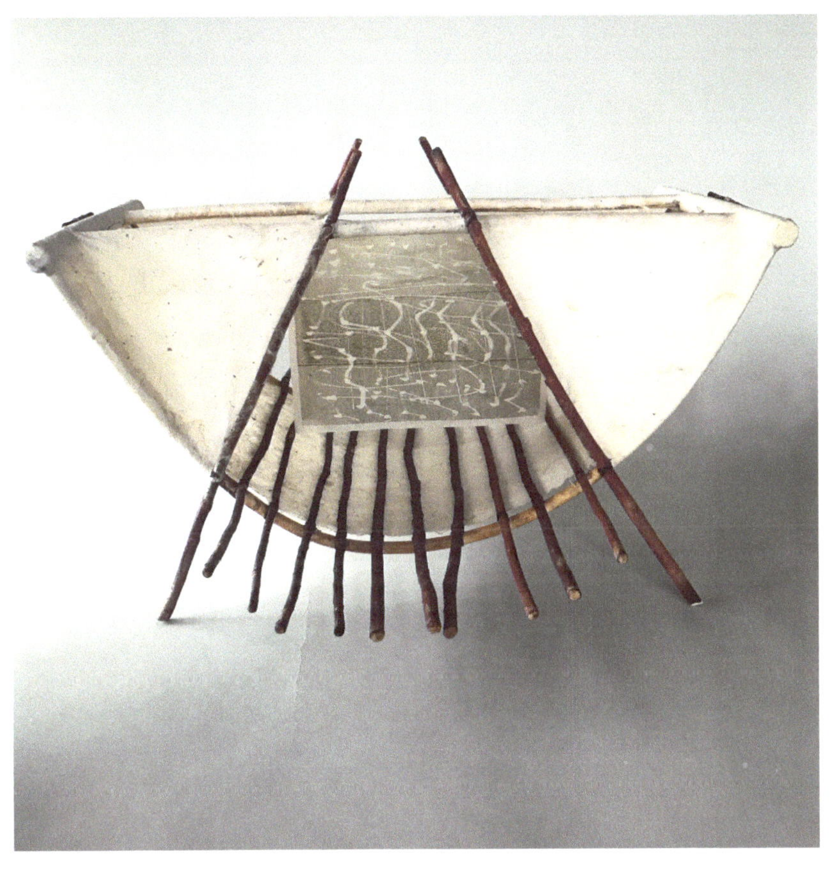

12.5.16 :: prayer for abigail

it's a girl, abi!
she whispers her name
from her mother's womb

she is her father's joy
we love her

come into this world
with the wisdom of your
past lives
for your parents
and all beings

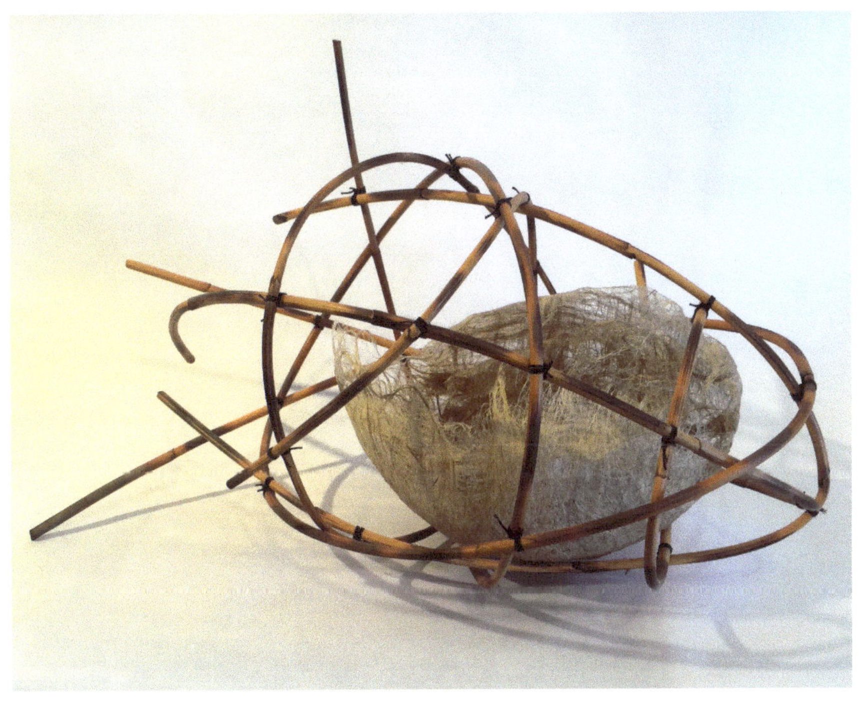

cocoon • *rattan, cast flax* • 2016

12.17.16

snowing sleet and wind
suffering in the unknown
wild birds visit

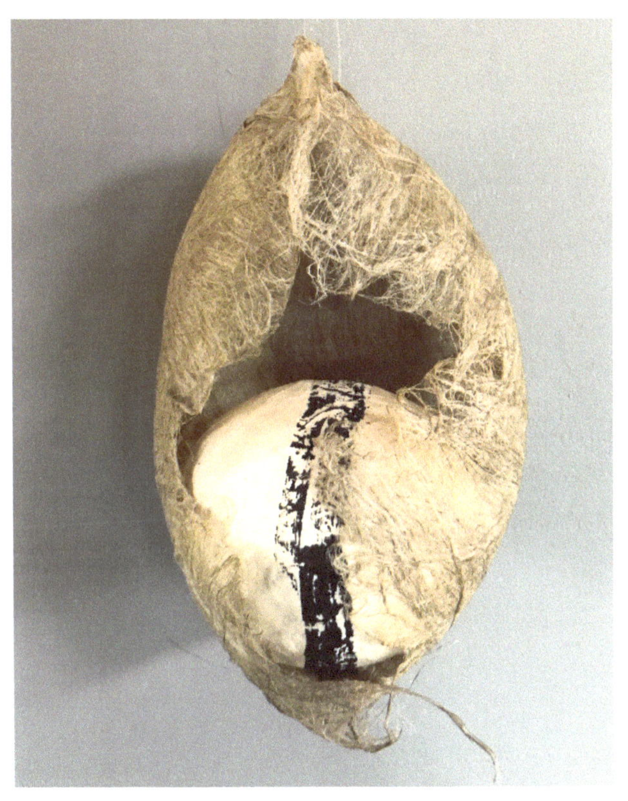

waiting • *flax, cast paper, ink* • 2016

12.22.16

snowflakes on the roof
sounds like rain birds piano
moving toward the light

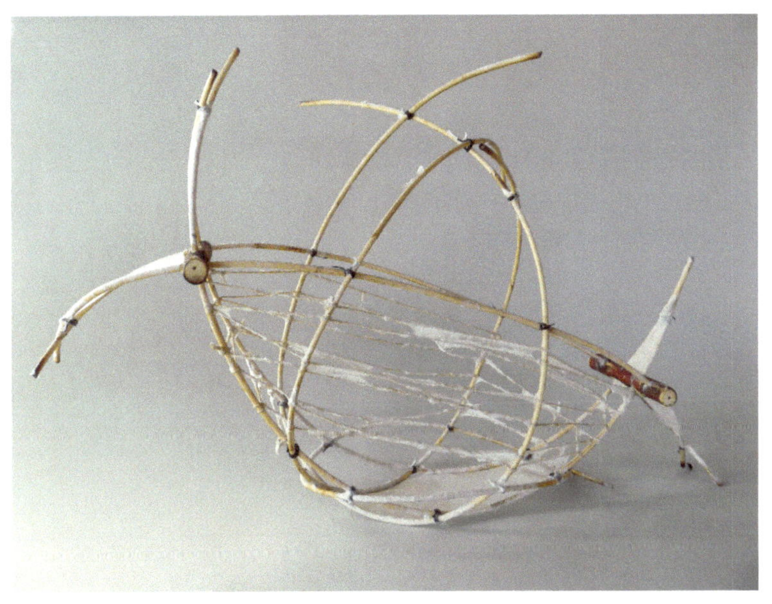

bird song • *rattan, pulp, waxed linen* • 2015

12.18.16 :: journey with hawthorn

tree of life
winter branches in vast landscape
meadow
horizon line

female figure in white flowing
gauze silk
she invites me to sit at the
base of the tree
she bathes me in white light
with her shawl

she gently touches and
strokes my left rib cage and thigh
she releases the pain
stored in those places for so
many years

betrayal

the tree becomes joyful with
white fragrant flowers
like tiny dancing stars

I make boats
they are my passage
to the underworld

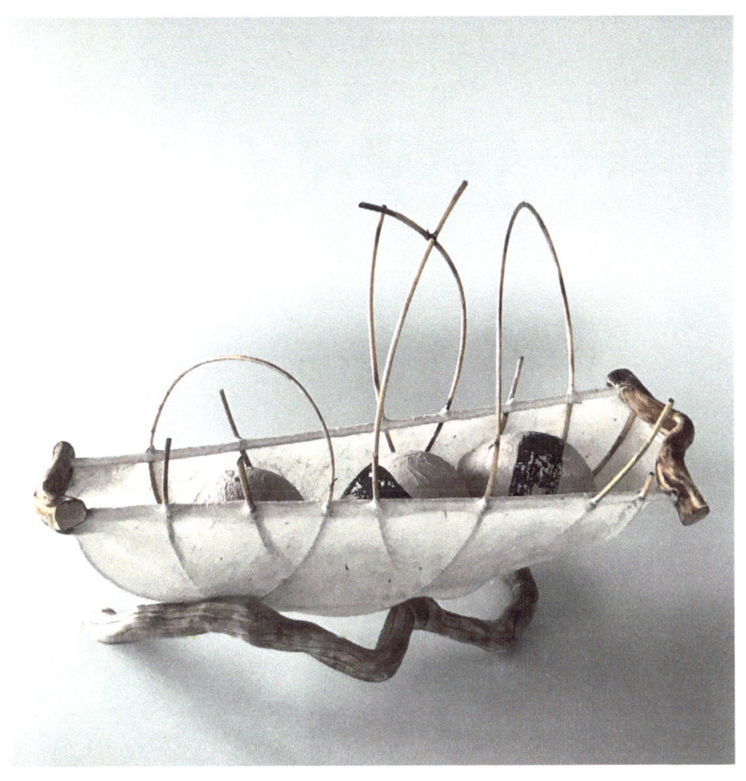

journey • *rattan, juniper wood, ink, cast paper, waxed linen* • 2016

12.28.16 :: a prayer for morgan

the crossroads appear
aside the parade passes
see you on the path

papa would say “you made your bed,
now sleep in it”
without an antidote

I have one
whatever lessons life brings
may you offer them to the
light for yourself and all beings

“you made your bed, now sleep in it”
I will always be here for you

the crossroad is appearing
I stand aside for the
parade of sleeping souls to pass
I choose a different path
the crossroad will come again
we will meet there

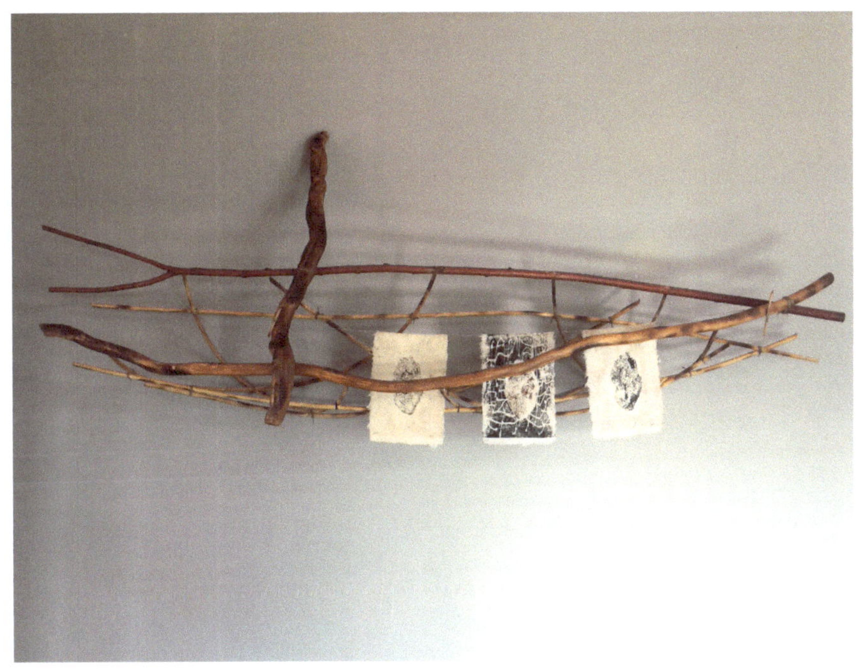

reflections from the bottom of the sea

juniper wood, rattan, monoprints on washi • 2016

1.5.17

snow sun clouds
turning a corner
beyond delusion
toward the light
and
another crossroad

going forward
only tracks behind

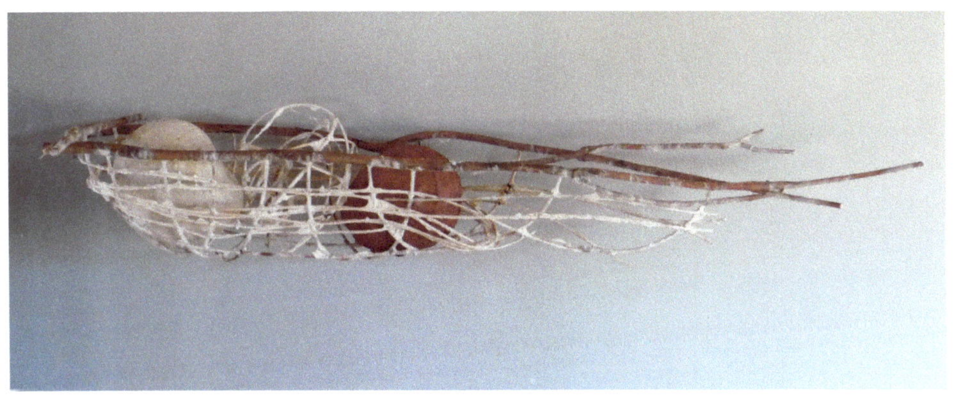

diviner • *willow, rattan, cast paper, pulp, waxed linen thread* • 2015

1.17.17

surface ripples clouds
georgia's mountain meets the lake
non duality

prayers for irene • *flax, wire, cast paper, ink, kakishibu* • 2016

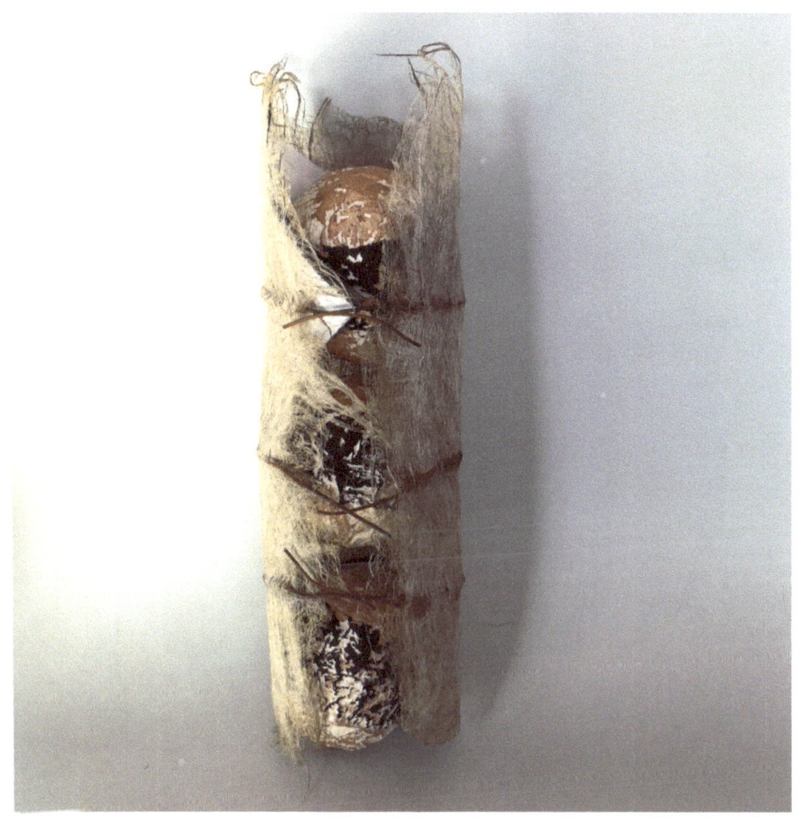

2.3.17

one little duck swims
smooth glass water reflects
mountains
trail left behind

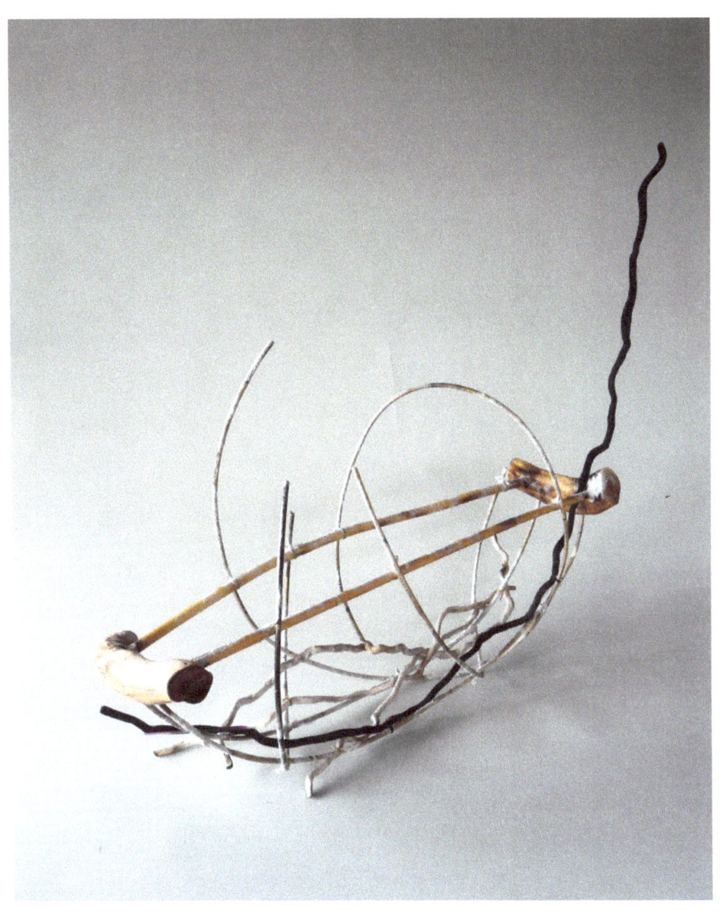

siren's song • *rattan, juniper wood, waxed linen thread* • 2015

jacqueline mallegni is an internationally recognized artist who creates mixed media minimalist sculpture. her focus is on the concept of "the spaces between" — between us and them, inside and outside, contemplation and chaos.

mallegni's sculptures are small installations made with rattan, foraged natural materials, Japanese-style handmade paper, cast flax, and silk roving fiber, and embellished with monoprints infused with sumi ink. her intention is to evoke a sense of place, to explore one's relationship to that place, and to pause and reflect on the beauty within. her work is ethereal in nature, inspired by Asian aesthetics and philosophies of wabi-sabi — acceptance of transience and imperfection, and yugen — deep awareness.

mallegni is a native of san francisco. she teaches workshops in california and new mexico; is a member of the surface design association, new mexico fiber artists directory, american craft council, international association of hand papermakers and paper artists; and is affiliated with inart gallery (santa fe, new mexico) and made contemporary craft (stinson beach, california). her work has been published in *still point arts quarterly* and *west marin review.*

www.mallegni.com • j.mallegni@gmail.com

www.ingramcontent.com/pod-product-compliance
Lightning Source LLC
LaVergne TN
LVHW070222110826
845147LV00003B/624

* 9 7 8 1 9 4 7 0 6 7 2 7 1 *